YOUR KNOWLEDGE HAS VALUE

- We will publish your bachelor's and master's thesis, essays and papers

- Your own eBook and book - sold worldwide in all relevant shops

- Earn money with each sale

Upload your text at www.GRIN.com
and publish for free

Bibliographic information published by the German National Library:

The German National Library lists this publication in the National Bibliography; detailed bibliographic data are available on the Internet at http://dnb.dnb.de .

Imprint:

Copyright © 2019 GRIN Verlag
Print and binding: Books on Demand GmbH, Norderstedt Germany
ISBN: 9783668953673

This book at GRIN:

https://www.grin.com/document/462230

Hisham Yahya

The Translation of Mus'id and Mus'ida's "The Gat" as an Arabic Source Text into English

Within the Framework of Theories and Strategies in Translation

GRIN Verlag

GRIN - Your knowledge has value

Since its foundation in 1998, GRIN has specialized in publishing academic texts by students, college teachers and other academics as e-book and printed book. The website www.grin.com is an ideal platform for presenting term papers, final papers, scientific essays, dissertations and specialist books.

Visit us on the internet:

http://www.grin.com/

http://www.facebook.com/grincom

http://www.twitter.com/grin_com

The Translation of Mus'id and Mus'ida's "The Gat" as an Arabic Source Text into English as a Target Text, Within the Framework of Theories and Strategies in Translation

1. An Introduction

Translating cultures is one of the most difficult tasks for translators. Due to numerous differences of cultures that's caused by language, differences may occur at the level of the word and above the level of the word as well. It is not surprising if a word may connote a different thing in one context, and the same time it connotes another thing in another context. Culturally speaking, the same word may connote a certain meaning in one culture while has different connotations in another culture. All that is due to certain reasons ascribed to ideology, attitude, association, pragmatics, or otherwise expressed. Hall (1976) presents an analogy that culture is similar to an iceberg. He proposed that 10% of the culture (external or surface culture) is easily visible like the tip of the iceberg such as food, clothing, art, dance etc, while 90%, of culture (internal or deep culture) is hidden below the surface like idiom, collocation, proverbs, metaphor and other figurative speech. To illustrate, the source text is from the Middle East Culture, especially from the traditionally Yemeni culture (Mus'id and Mus'ida Broadcasting), needs to be transferred into totally different culture (Western Culture). The translator has to bridge the gap by using strategies like Foreignization and Demostication, to reach the main purpose of the ST.

The purpose of the current text is to acquaint the target reader about the new culture which is not found there in the target culture. To illustrate, the source text is a mixture of socio-cultural habituations, constructed within the Arabic underlined by Sana'ni Dialect (genre shift). Thus, revealing such merged discourse and transfer it the way the ST requires is absolutely a tough task for any translator, many tools (Methods and Strategies such as Skopos Theory, Saussure's Signifier and Signifier, Baker's Translating Idiomatic Expressions and Venuti's Foreignization and Domestication.) of translation should be tackled during the process of translation.

According to Translation Studies and Approaches, there are not theoretical models of translation to solve all the problems a translator encounters, instead, theories should formulate a set of strategies for approaching problems and for coordinating the different aspects entailed. In the following analysis, it is our intention to examine the functionality (the Skopos) of the source spoken texts produced for the English Speakers, especially the American and British people. Since the Skopos Theory meets the growing need for non-literary translation in the latter half of the twentieth century (Schäffner, 1998:235).

2. The literature Review

2.1 A Brief Outline of Cultural Translation

In field of translation, there has been a long hot debate over the proper translation strategy chosen for the transmission of cultural contents. Since a publicity text is "content-focused" rather than "form-focused" (Reiss 2000), the translator should transmit the ST's conceptual content and does not have to preserve the ST's linguistic form or original style insofar as the TT fulfills its intended skopos or function. Most cultural words are easy to detect, since they are associated with a particular language cannot be literally translated, but many cultural customs are described in ordinary language. So it was worthy to find the most adequate theory of translation to adequate the TT culture not to accurate the ST. According to Nord (1997: 47-48), s/he must adhere to the principle of loyalty, which has two directions: towards the ST, and towards the TT reader. Nord, stressing the concept of loyalty, considers that the translator's task is to "mediate" between the two cultures without falling into the trap of "cultural imperialism", i.e. without pretending that the concept of culture A is superior and, therefore, must be adopted by others.

2.2 A Brief Outline of the Skopos Theory

The Skopos Theory was developed in Germany in the late 1970s. Since it reflects a general shift from linguistic and formal translation theories to a more functionally and socio-culturally oriented concept of translation, it has become "a welcome addition to translation studies" (Gentzler 2001:71). Initially formulated by Reiss in the 1970s, the theory was enunciated by Vermeer in the 1980s, and was further developed in the 1990s by Nord, one of its most important second-generation scholars. The basic principles of the Skopos Theory are summarized as follows:

Any form of translational action, including translation itself, may be conceived as a "purposeful activity" (Nord 1997:12). The action should observe the "skopos rule," which postulates that the form of a target text (TT), including translation strategies and methods adopted, should above all be determined by the purpose or skopos that the TT is intended to fulfill in the target context; that is, "the end justifies the means" (Reiss and Vermeer 1984:101). Proponents of this approach maintain that it is the 'skopos' or purpose of a translation, and the manner and degree to which target culture norms are treated or ignored in a translation which are of overriding importance for translator to take them into account during rendering.(Reiss and Vermeer 1984)

A distinction is made by Reiss and Vermeer (1984) between equivalence and adequacy in translation. Equivalence in Reiss and Vermeer's view refers to the relationship between an original and its translation whenever both fulfill the same communicative function, and adequacy is the relationship between an original and a translation where no functional match is obtained, and where the "Skopos" of the translation has been consistently attended to. Therefore, Skopos Theory was found as the best approach to approach the cultural gap of both Yemeni and Western Cultures. Throughout the whole text, the main purpose of such analysis is to transfer the strange culture (ST) to the (TT) readers. Another purpose is to persuade the readers as the 'cause-effect relations'. To translate the current text according to Skopos theory, we should take into account certain rules during translation; the skopos rule, the fidelity rule, the coherence rule, and the loyalty principle are proposed to guide translators in their translation process.

2.3 Baker's Strategies to Overcome the Difficulties of Idiomatic Translation

Translating idioms has always been a challenging decision-making process for translators mainly because not all idioms have direct equivalents in the target language. According to Baker (1992) nonequivalence may be at the level of word or above it. Nonequivalence at word level can occur because of the absence in the target culture of a relevant situational feature for the source language text (Bassnett, 1980:39). This is because the concept may be lexicalized in the SL and not in the TL. Sapir and Whorf (1964) have best illustrated this phenomenon through giving the example of "snow". European countries have many words for snow because it falls many times in the year, in contrast to other countries, like Arab ones, that lexicalize only one type of snow. This phenomenon is highly related to culture. Baker (1992, p. 65) claims that "the first difficulty that a translator comes across is being able to recognize that s/he is dealing with an idiomatic expression". She believes that some of the idiomatic expressions are recognized more easily than some other ones mentioning two situations in which an expression can be recognized easily:

1) When the idioms "violate truth conditions", and
2) When the idioms include expressions which seem grammatically "ill-formed".

In addition, Baker (1992) throughout the part and pages regarding difficulties of translating idiomatic expressions classifies these problems into four subcategories:

1) An idiom or fixed expression may have no equivalent in the target language.

2) An idiom or fixed expression may have a similar counterpart in the target language, but its context of use may be different.
3) An idiom may be used in the source text in both its literal and idiomatic senses at the same time.
4) The very convention of using idioms in written discourse, the contexts in which they can be used, and their frequency of use may be different in the source and target languages (pp. 65-71).

Although there are some difficulties in the process of translating idioms and fixed expressions, on the other hand there are some strategies to overcome such probable difficulties. Baker (1992) declares four problem-solving strategies considering this issue as follows:

1) Using an idiom of similar meaning and form.
2) Using an idiom of similar meaning but dissimilar form
3) Translation by paraphrase
4) Translation by omission (pp. 71-78).

Moreover, she states that:

"The way in which an idiom or a fixed expression can be translated into another language depends on many factors....Questions of style, register, and rhetorical effect must also be taken into consideration" *(ibid: 71-72).*

Finally, Fernando and Flavell (1981, p. 82) warn translators against "the strong unconscious urge in most translators to search hard for an idiom in the receptor language, however inappropriate it may be" (Cited in Baker, 1992,p. 72).

2.4 Genre Analysis

The linguistic style used in such texts is colloquial. Genre refers to the conventional text type that is associated with a specific communicative function. The genre type used in the source text is different from the genre used in the target text analysis; the source text genre is dialectical while in the target text is written one. It's persuasive in the source text while informative in the target one. Genre connects texts with the 'macro-context' i.e. the Context of Cultures of the linguistic and cultural community in which the text is embedded. Due to the depth culture of the source spoken text, and to the huge gap of both cultures, the need was necessary to use many strategies to help the translator to adequate the source text culture into the target language culture. Combination of strategies or as Mailhac called it "combination of procedures "means to use more than one strategy or method to facilitate the translation process (Mailhac, 1996 p. 141). Dickins et al. (2002, p. 177) point out that "the term 'text-type' is often used in a similar sense to 'genre'. Then they define genre as "a category to which, in a given culture, a given text is seen to belong, and within which the text is seen to share a type of communicative purpose and effect with other texts; that is, the text is seen to be more or less typical of the genre)"ibid, p. 236). The text -type belongs to the old Yemeni folklore that deal with the problem of youth chewing Qat, to be addicted to such kind of drugs. For the Western Culture, such cultural differences may be difficult for the translator to translate directly without considering the 'the Context of Cultures' Thus, many strategies should be utilized to transfer the massage properly such as foreignization, addition, omission, definition and explanation.

2.5 Ferdinand de Saussure's signifier and signified

Newmark (1988: 94) suggests that culture is "the way of life and its manifestations that are peculiar to a community that uses a particular language as its means of expression''. Saussure's the signified and signifier were purely psychological; they were form rather than substance. Today, following Hjelmslev, the signifier is interpreted as the material form (something which can be seen, heard, touched, smelled or tasted) and the signified as the mental concept (Chandler,2017, pp14). In addition to that, Rohner (1984), states that culture is "a system of symbolic meanings that shape one's way of thinking". Contextually speaking, the word "bondug " which refers to 'peace' in the source text context; Sometimes "gun" according to Yemeni customs (the tribal manner) can be laid down by two quarreled parties and given to an agreed person to solve their problem, while has different reference in the target text context. The term "gat" refers to the target reader with various connotations mostly positive while in the target reader understanding is mostly close to bad side of it (addiction equals Heroin). The sayings and proverbs mentioned in the text are contextualized in metaphor. Although the reference is more literary than linguistic, the import of the interactional nature of proverbs, its universal and experiential relevance are notable. In a similar way to proverbs all over the world, Sana'ni proverbs are products of the people's socio-cultural and geographical experience. In other words, they are used to express the forms and the situation, flora and fauna of the people according to their natural environment. The experimental reality of the Sana'ni proverbs is different from those of other language groups whose geographical and socio-cultural realities differ. Proverbs are used therefore by the Yemeni people not only as a vehicle of the expression of truth, religion, morality but also dominant occupation, and other practices which reflect their day-to-day living.

3. A brief outline of the Mus'id and Mus'ida Broadcasting

"Mus'id wi Mus'idah" was a daily program broadcasted from Sana'a's radio in 1988, presented by Abdurrahman Muttahar and Habiba Mohammed. It was a simple, instructional, dialectical, Yemeni radio broadcast. It is used to deal with social and family issues. It had a wide range of audience among the Yemeni society because it handled some social problems and issues in a sarcastic and funny way. It was presented in a Sana'ani dialect so that it became close to all Yemeni people especially those who speak Sana'ani dialect. The musical song of the introduction was concerned with a social work, a wife and an alimen. The idea of the program was created by Abdulrahman Mutahher who created such characters close to Yemeni society; "Mus'id" and "Mus'idah". The program depended on the idea that both characters had the responsibility to solve the whole problems of the family initially the problems of healthcare then developed to handle many social problems.

4. The Transcription of "GAT"

Ma: Since you are the one who got your sons hooked on gat[1], you'll have to feed their habit to supply their gat Willy-nilly. It's a real battle to give up an entrenched habit!

M: I no longer know who I am battling with and who's in my side!

Ma If your picket's full[2], it's in your side; and if you pocket is empty, you can't even bank on your children being on your side!

M: What a good speaker you become! there are no flies on you![3] and all this time I'd thought you were an innocent!.

Ma: I don't know how to talk well! the only innocent around here is you! You get your sons hooked on gat, and now that they're hooked you go and attack them ! because they still chew.! there is no point, Mus'ida!.

---

[1]- Qat is pronounced as gat in Sanani Dialect and it is a type of grass that Yemeni people used to chew with. According to Wikipedia: " is a flowering plant native to the Horn of Africa and the Arabian Peninsula. Khat contains the alkaloid cathinone, a stimulant, which is said to cause excitement, loss of appetite, and euphoria. Among communities from the areas where the plant is native, khat chewing has a history as a social custom dating back thousands of years analogous to the use of coca leaves in South America and betel nut in Asia. The World Health Organization (WHO) classified it in 1980 as a drug of abuse that can produce psychological dependence".

[2] - If you are rich

[3]- It's an equivalent for the source spoken text ' masha' allah alleik'. According to Cambridge English Dictionary, " *no flies* on sb definition: If *you* say *there are no flies* on someone, *you* mean that they cannot easily be deceived", in which considered as the same as the connotative meaning of the source speaker.

M: It's not up to me to supply them with gat so they can chew. I'm only supposed to supply them with food!

Ma: Why didn't you just leave at that, then? What on earth made you get them addicted to gat?

M: It's your fault! You're the one who made them addicted.

Ma: Stop trying to shift the blame and run away from facts! If you don't, you lay down your gun and I'll lay down mine[4] and we'll sort this out in a proper tribal manner.

M: What good would that do? I've already sold my gun to pay for your sons' gat- and you haven't got a gun, and would not even know to fire one if you had!

Ma: So now what should we do? You'd better have a look around for things to sell or pawn. Your sons are totally hooked. They don't seem to have any purpose in live other than their bag with gat. 'They dropped me in the sea of passion and left me, though my rope measured no more than a yard.'[5] And Mus'id, would no skill whatsoever, manages to get his son addicted to gat.

M: Mus'ida! Now what?

M: I went over to see my uncle and complain to him about my sons. I told him that they weren't studying properly and they wouldn't stay at home. I'd started to worry about them wondering about the streets and the souk. He told me that 'the only thing that would

---

[4] According to Yemeni tribal manner, people sometime resort to solve their own problems by laying 'guns' (both conflict sides), giving them into a chosen tribal judge to solve their problems.

[5] when she was very little.

keep them at home and help them to study was gat'. He said , 'Give them a little gat to stop them wondering around the souk'![6] I had absolutely no idea, Muse'ida, that they would become so addicted they'd start looking around for things to sell and pawn.

Ma: Fine! "Face the music"! I want nothing to do with it! I'm telling you, your sons are interested in nothing but their bag of gat even if it means sleeping on the streets to get it![7]

M: What should I do? I've tried all possible ways to convince them of the harmful effects of gat, in terms of money, health and particularly the effect on the family's income and the pure west of time.

Ma: What did they say when you told them all that?

M: Oh stop it! You don't want to know!

Ma: What don't i want to know?

M: Oh very well! They said, 'will give up chewing the moment you and all the other dads, Dad! It's not right for you to continue chewing gat when we can't'.

Ma: Did they really say that to you, or are you making it up?

---

[6] As contributed in Yemeni society especially who are addicted to Qat that a qat chewer stay stick to the place where s/he is chewing in, enjoying the taste of qat and that as a reflection of qat chewing.

[7] Metaphorically speaking, due to the addiction of qat, a qat chewer does everything to get qat.

M: Why on earth should I make it up? They also told me that the taste and effect of gat is so cool that once you've tasted it you'll go back for more!

Ma: Where are these cool effects of gat when you can see your toes sticking out of your shoes? You can't buy another pair because of the gat! Then the store room door's broken, and the windows of my room are smashed, and the telephone's cut off and they are about to remove the line all together. We only ever buy chicken when we know someone's coming for lunch, so that they don't go around saying we don't eat anything as a result of gat!

M: Mus'id!

Ma: What is it now?

M: Don't shout at me and don't go around clucking like a mother hen! At first, I was the only gat addicted. Then, I let my sons try it and now there are five of us. Whatever money we have, we use for the bus or a motorbike to go straight to the gat souk. Don't you see, Mus'ida? All the valleys and fields and farmland has been set aside for gat. The amount of gat brought from the countryside to the towns increases at the same rate as the amount of land set aside for gat. The main economic and social activity takes place in that gat souk. You will find everyone at the gat souk – from grandfathers and fathers down grandsons once they've reached the age of fifteen. And I'll tell this, Mus'ida, the gat problem won't go away until God brings in a generation which is absolutely convinced of the harmful effects of gat, and then uproots the gat bushes which themselves uprooted the coffee trees and all the fruit trees used to have!

5. The Analysis of the Radio Play

The purpose of the original text is to tell the audience about the problems and symptoms of chewing qat (quit chewing qat and addiction).therefore, the purpose of the original is persuasive, while the purpose of the target text would be informative because the current issue of chewing qat only found in the original culture while is not there in the culture of the target audience.

In addition to that, the cultural differences between both counterparts; Arabic and English one is full of problems. The most cultural problematic factors the translator may hinder in translating the current discourse such as; collocations, proverbs and sayings, semiotics…etc. The cultural gap may occur during rendering the source text discourse that causes the target reader misunderstands the original meaning. In other words, what seems sense for the ST reader, it may be nonsense for the TT reader. Ilyas (1989:128) points out that words which have various connotations in one language may not have the same emotive associations in another context such as the word "Bundog". Different languages frequently reflect different connotations and associations of feeling because of the differences in cultural roots. That's why Ilyas states:

A translator of English-Arabic texts may come across some problematic ecological-based idioms and expressions. Some such items acquire different connotations in both languages. What may be a connotatively favorable expression in Arabic could have a pejorative sense in English, and vice versa.

(Ilyas, 1989: 128)

5.1 Vocabulary

Throughout the whole transcription of Mus'id and Mus'ida play, the translator confronts with many challenges to render cultural and linguistic gaps in rendering sayings and proverbs, norms and conventions, habits and customs which have no place in the target culture. The broadcasting program is totally directed towards the Yemeni citizens dealing with certain social issues such as the current issue of youth chewing Qat,; spending time and money. Thus, the wording of the text have been structured and arranged a way that fits the context of the source culture. To look for something fits the source culture in the target culture for example terms like; "Gat", "Bundog", "Mudmin". To illustrate, the target reader refers quickly to the 'addiction' of drugs according to their own pre-knowledge about DRUGS. You as a translator, you have to render the source culture into the target one, using the techniques of Freignization and Explanation. The translation by the latter strategy is to transfer a new culture into the target reader's culture. So, the translator has to render such issues somehow literally, aiming into the target reader's understanding regarding the connotative meaning of the source language speakers.

5.2 Sayings and Proverbs

During the process of translation, the translator uses idiomatic language and the technique of substitution to give the complete sense of meanings, show the hidden meanings and for cultural influence. For Sayings and Proverbs which have equivalence in the target language literature, such as the source language idiom, "asidaq matineh' is substituted by a close saying in the target culture, "face the music". Some others are translated literary such as the ST Saying, "etha gaybak malan …….we etha gaybak atal…….", Could be translated a: " If your picket's full, it's in your side; and if you pocket is empty, you can't even bank on your children being on your side!."

5.3 Cultural Differences

Another hindrance the translator may hinder during the process of rendering is certain social customs and habits such as the source language Saying, "etrahi bondug wana atrah bondug"; such saying is circulated in Yemen especially in Northern Yemen such as Sana'a, Ammran, and etc. Sana'a, where the Play is produced, people sometime resort to solve their own problems by laying 'guns' (both conflict sides), giving them into a chosen tribal judge to solve their problems. Such cultural gap cannot be found in the target one and has no equivalence in the target culture as well. Such strategy of translation is referred to by Venuti's Foreignization and Demostication (1995/2008). The term "Gat" is new to the knowledge and the understanding of target Language reader so, such new terms should be rendered by 'definition' and' explanation'.

Taking into account 'the culture of context', what concern Mus'id and Mus'ida as parents is not physical and mental symptoms which may be caused due to chewing qat, but the financial harms. In the other hand, the target readers may understand the term "Qat" as a type of drugs as Cocaine according to the their pre-knowledge of the term 'addiction'. The translator in such cases has to render the source text terms, "wala'tahom" into "addicted them" with explaining. Thus, the translator has to be aware of rendering such issues by taking into account the most equivalent strategy to render such misunderstanding. According to the 'culture of context', the translator has to be aware of rendering such issues, taking into account the connotations of such words that carry on different connotations in the target context such as the source text "mudmin qat" and "masha' allah alleik" has totally different connotations in the context of the western culture. The translator may resort to render such cultural differences using adequate words that have the same meaning as the original one such as (hooked, addicted= mudmin qat).

6. The Conclusion

The current work of Mus'id wa Mus'ida "the Gat" is full of culture-specific elements, dialectical expressions and norms that are totally different from those found in Western Culture. To bridge the cultural gap, many techniques and strategies used to present the possibility of translating cultures; dialectical expressions, culture-specific elements and norms. The source text is persuasive; telling the audience about certain issue of the bad habit of chewing qat that leads to poverty (as the main problem in Yemen) and giving them the solutions for such problems. To render a foreign culture, the target text would be informative; the target reader receives new norms and information. Foreinization and Demostication are considered as good strategies for translators to render cultural differences.

7. References

Hall, E. T. (1976). Beyond culture. New York: Doubleday.

Munday, J. (2001). Introducing Translation Studies: Theories and Applications. London: Routledge.

Schäffner, C. (1998). "Skopos theory." In M. Baker (ed.). Routledge Encyclopedia of Translation Studies. London and New York: Routledge, 235-238.

Nord, C. (1991a). "Scopos, loyalty and translational conventions." Target, 3 (1): 91-109. (1991b). Text Analysis in Translation. Amsterdam: Rodopi. (1997). Translating as a Purposeful Activity: Functionalist Approaches Explained. Manchester: St. Jerome.

Reiss, K. and Hans J. Vermeer. (1984). Grundlegung einer allgemeinen Translationstheorie. Tübingen: Niemeyer.

Bassnet, S. (1991) Translation Studies. London: Routledge. Carter, R. (1993). Introducing Applied Linguistics. London: Penguin books.

Sapir, E. and Whorf, B. (1964) American Anthropologist. United States of America.

Newmark, P. (2003) A Text Book of Translayion. Edinburgh: Pearson Education limited.

Baker, M (1992). In Other Words: A Course Book on Translation. London: Routledge.

Chandler, Daniel (2017). Semiotics: The Basics, New York: Routledge

Rohner, R.P. (1984). Toward a Conception of Culture for Cross-Cultural Psychology. Journal of Cross-cultural psychology. 15 (2): pp. 111-138.

Dickins, J., Hervey, S., & Higgins, I. (2002). Thinking Arabic Translation. London: Routledge.

Ilyas, A. (1989). Theories of Translation. Mowsil: University of Mowsil.

YOUR KNOWLEDGE HAS VALUE